# CONTENTS





Words that look like <u>this</u> can be found in the glossary on page 24.

# SUPER START!

Science is a way of finding out about our universe by looking closely at things, asking questions, and trying out ideas. We can do experiments to find out how things work, grow, move, and change.

SUPER SCIENCE

# ANIMALS

WRITTEN BY

Valerie Harvey

KidHaven PUBLISHING

Published in 2027 by
KidHaven Publishing, an Imprint of Greenhaven Publishing, LLC
2544 Clinton St., Buffalo, NY 14224



**Written by:** Valerie Harvey
**Edited by:** Nicola Chave
**Designed by:** Lucy Otter



**Cataloging-in-Publication Data**

Names: Harvey, Valerie.
Title: Animals / Valerie Harvey.
Description: Buffalo, NY : KidHaven Publishing, 2027. | Series: Super science | Includes glossary and index.
Identifiers: ISBN 9781534570498 (pbk.) | ISBN 9781534570504 (library bound) | ISBN 9781534570511 (ebook)
Subjects: LCSH: Animals--Juvenile literature.
Classification: LCC QL49.H378 2027 | DDC 590--dc23



Printed in China

CPSIA compliance information: Batch #QS27KH: For further information contact Greenhaven Publishing LLC at 1-844-317-7404.

Please visit our website, www.greenhavenpublishing.com.
For a free color catalog of all our high-quality books, call toll free 1-844-317-7404 or fax 1-844-317-7405.

Find us on

Image Credits. All images courtesy of Shutterstock.com, unless otherwise stated.
Cover – Dragon Images. Recurring – Leremy, Dedraw Studio. Cover – Anna Zhukkova 4–5 – Hero Images. 6–7 – AB Photo Master, biletskiyevgeniy.com, Jamikorn Sooktaramorn, KensCanning. 8–9 – Candra gubta, GagliardiPhotography, HoneyLinn, I Wayan Sumatika, un.bolovan. 10–11 – Bachkova Natalia, CassandraSm, Stephan Morris, Wirestock Creators. 12–13 – dogaergun, Martin Prochazkacz, Wailani. 14–15 – A. Emson, Abu Bakar official, Nick Greaves, Rogue Productions LLC. 16–17 – Daniel Prudek, W. de Vries, WildMedia. 18–19 – Andreas Vogel, Hawatrending, Robert Schneider, Vladislav Gajic 20–21 – 24K-Production, Eric Isslee, NassornSnitwong.

Say hello to Captain Curious! Captain Curious is on a mission to learn about animals of every shape and size. Together, we are going to uncover amazing facts about some of the world's furry, scaly, and feathered animals.

# AMAZING ANIMALS

Animals are incredible creatures with special powers that help them survive. Some can run fast, some can fly, and some are very good at hiding.

Animals live in oceans, forests, deserts, and even our homes. Animals have adaptations that help them to stay safe, find food, have babies, and move around the places they live. Adaptations are a bit like superpowers!

Animals live on all our continents.

# MEET THE MAMMALS

Mammals are warm-blooded animals. Some mammals are big and some are very small. All mammals breathe air, and most have hair or fur that covers their bodies.

Humans are mammals, too!

Not all mammals look the same, and they can live in very different places. Some even live underwater! Some mammals can run quickly, others can swim, and a few can glide through the trees.

# MEET THE BIRDS

Birds are the sky's feathered superheroes. Their feathers keep them warm and help them fly, glide, and soar high above the ground. Birds lay eggs and build nests to keep them safe.

This peregrine falcon is looking after her chicks.

Some birds sing beautiful songs. Some have brightly colored feathers that help them show off, while others have feathers that help them blend in with their habitat.

A FEW BIRDS, SUCH AS PENGUINS, OSTRICHES, AND EMUS, HAVE FEATHERS BUT CANNOT FLY.

# MEET THE FISH

Fish are underwater champions. Their fins and smooth bodies help them swim through the water. They have gills that let them breathe without needing to come up for air.

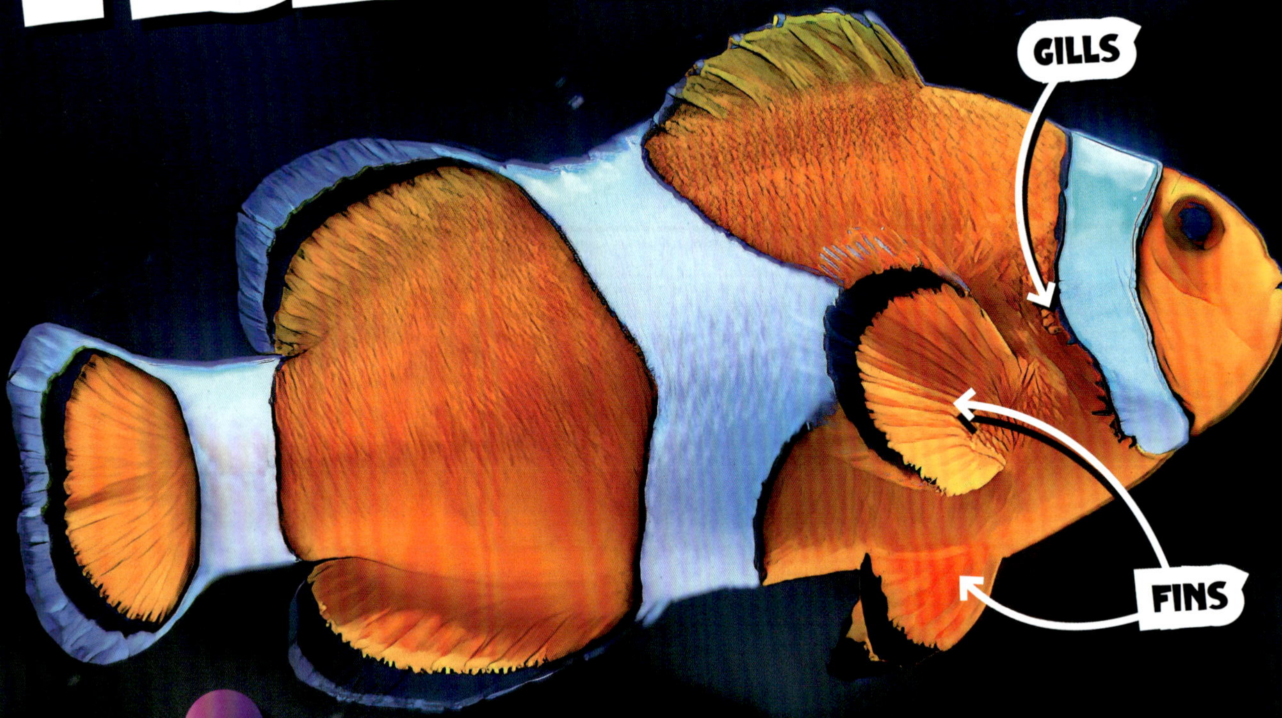


A group of fish is called a shoal.

Fish come in all shapes and sizes, from tiny minnows to huge sharks. Some live in fresh water, such as lakes and rivers. Others live in the salty ocean.

Most types of fish lay eggs!

# MEET THE REPTILES

Reptiles are scaly, cold-blooded animals that love warm places. They breathe air, lay eggs, and often bask in sunlight to warm up.

Snakes, lizards, turtles, and crocodiles are all reptiles. Their tough scales protect them, giving them super-armor. After a while, they shed their old skin to reveal fresh, new skin underneath.

Reptiles are tough!

# MEET THE AMPHIBIANS

Amphibians are cold-blooded animals that have two different lives—one in water and one on land. Frogs, toads, and salamanders hatch from eggs in the water and later grow legs to hop or walk on land.

When amphibians are young, they use gills to breathe underwater. As they get older, they grow lungs that let them breathe in air.

# MEET THE INSECTS

Insects are tiny but mighty superheroes of the natural world. All insects have six legs. Lots of them have hard shells and many have wings. Bees, butterflies, beetles, and ants are all insects.

Lots of insects are very good at working together. Some pollinate plants, some build tunnels, and others create amazing honeycombs! Their superpower is teamwork to solve big problems.

# MEET THE PETS

Pets are usually friendly animals that live with people. Dogs, cats, rabbits, fish, and more can all be wonderful <u>companions</u>. Humans take care of their pets with food, water, and love.

Some pets have special jobs that help people. Pets can help their owners with medical conditions, such as guide dogs that help people who are blind or cannot see well.

Pets can be super helpers!

# SUPER SCIENCE CHALLENGE

Are you ready to become a science superhero? Take this quiz and check your answers on page 23.

1. Mammals are warm-blooded and have hair or fur. (True/False)

2. Birds use their feathers to keep warm. (True/False)

3. Fish breathe air using lungs, just like humans. (True/False)

4. Reptiles have scales that protect their bodies. (True/False)

5. Insects always have eight legs. (True/False)

You have completed this Super Science book and have now become a

# ★ SCIENCE SUPERHERO! ★

Keep exploring, asking questions, and discovering amazing things about the world.

Answers:
1. True. 2. True. 3. False: Fish breathe with gills, not lungs. 4. True. 5. False: Insects have six legs.

# GLOSSARY

| | |
|---|---|
| **ADAPTATIONS** | ways animals have changed over time to suit their homes |
| **BASK** | to lie in a warm, light place |
| **COLD-BLOODED** | animals that have blood that changes with the temperature around them |
| **COMPANIONS** | people or animals that someone spends a lot of time with |
| **CONTINENTS** | large areas of land, such as Africa or Europe, that are typically made up of many countries |
| **EXPERIMENTS** | tests to work things out and find out new things about something |
| **POLLINATE** | to pass on pollen from a plant to a plant of the same kind, so that seeds will be produced |
| **SURVIVE** | to stay alive |
| **UNIVERSE** | all the planets, stars and moons that make up space |
| **WARM-BLOODED** | animals that have blood that stays at a steady and warm temperature |

# INDEX